ME, MY FRIEND
and the
MONSTER

A True Never-Ending Story

By *Tarif Youssef-Agha*

Developed & Edited By *Kathleen J. Shields*

ISBN-13: 978-1-941345-87-0

Illustrations by: Aashay Utkarsh

Canyon Lake, TX
www.ErinGoBraghPublishing.com

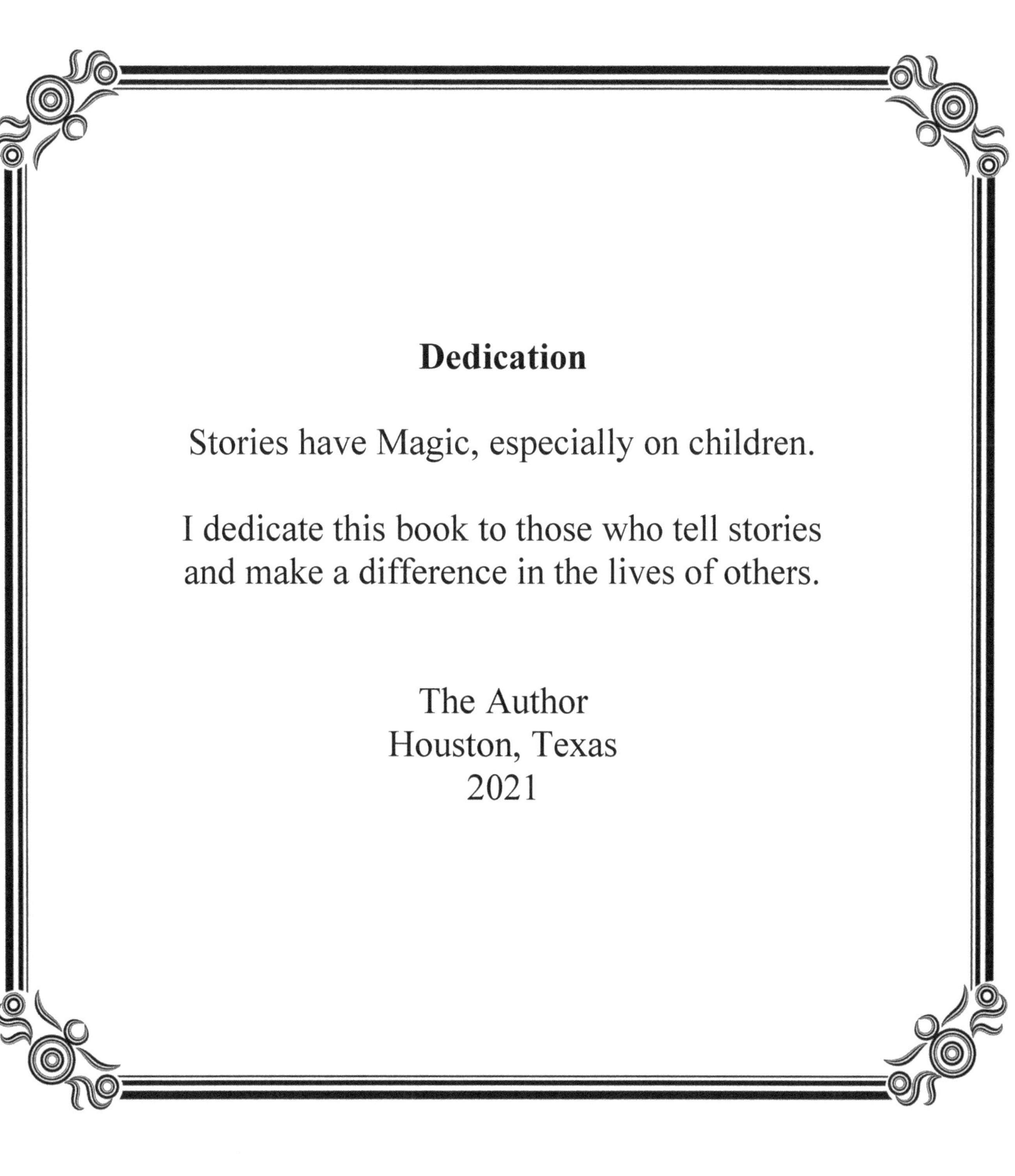

Dedication

Stories have Magic, especially on children.

I dedicate this book to those who tell stories
and make a difference in the lives of others.

The Author
Houston, Texas
2021

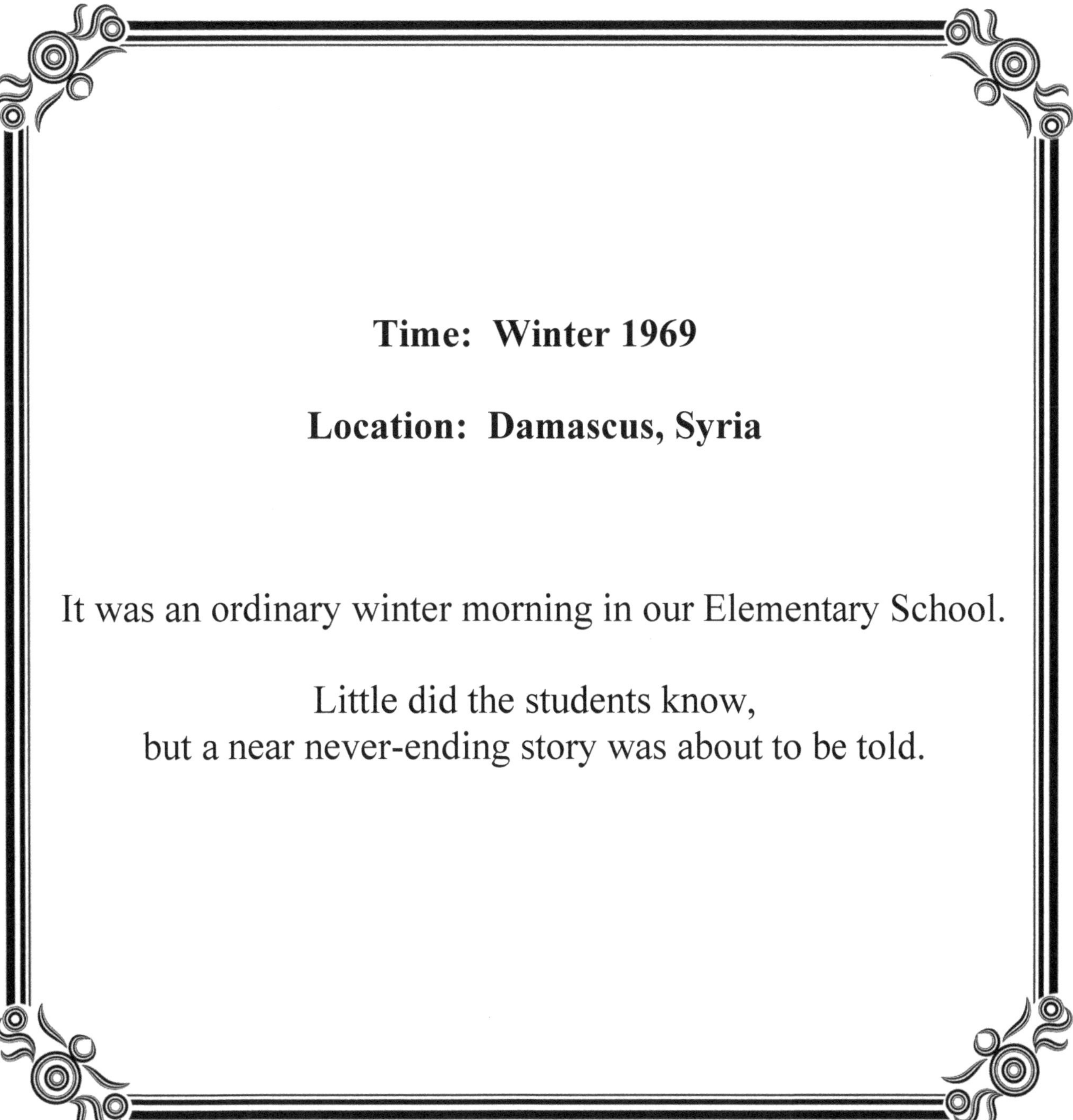
Time: Winter 1969

Location: Damascus, Syria

It was an ordinary winter morning in our Elementary School.

Little did the students know,
but a near never-ending story was about to be told.

Ten minutes into the class, a school janitor knocked at the classroom door, opened it slowly, and told the teacher that he was needed in the principal's office.

Since teachers couldn't leave children unsupervised in the classrooms, and since I was known to everyone in the school as a STORY TELLER, he assigned me to come forward to his desk and do what I do the best.

I always loved this kind of opportunity! I grew up a story-teller and enjoyed sharing my stories with my classmates. They enjoyed hearing my adventures and my teacher "won" a quiet class while he was away. It was a win-win-win.

Growing up, our Nanny used to tell us bedtime stories about Kings and Monsters, Magic Lamps, Genies, and Flying Rugs. Later in my youth, I thrilled in reading Comic Books like *Superman*, and *Batman*.

My favorite thing to do was to take all of the characters I got to know from books and merge them together to make my own stories.

In one story, *Aladdin* asked the help of a *Superman*, and in another one, *Batman* found himself fighting a monster with a Genie.

I remember one time a kid questioned my mix of characters. He said, "Hey, *Superman* and *Aladdin* shouldn't meet in one story because they live in different times, different worlds and speak different languages."

My response was, "If you are so smart, why don't you sit in my chair and be the narrator?" Everyone laughed and asked me to complete the story, including that kid.

I started that day's story as I always did "Once upon a time in a far, far land."

The story was a mix from *The Book of Arabian Nights*, and my own imagination. The hero was *Al-Shater Hassan*, or *Hassan the Magnificent*, whose character was similar to that of *Aladdin*.

He had a flying rug that he used in his journeys and adventures. I gave that magic carpet the name *'Aziza'* which meant 'The Dignified' in Arabic.

At one point in the story, *Hassan the Magnificent* was about to save a kidnapped *Princess,* but was trapped by a giant one-eye Ghoul, and taken to his cave to be eaten at dinner.

Aziza managed to follow them to the cave, but was attacked by the cave guard; a huge fire-spitting serpent with seven heads.

Aziza dodged the dangerous serpent heads and was just about to enter the cave when the serpent spit a fireball and set her fringe ablaze!

All students were frozen in their seats. All you could hear was pounding heart beats, as they held their breath waiting to find out what happened next. Would *Aziza* fight back to save her master? Would she catch on fire and turn to ash? The whole class was silently waiting.

I was just about to continue when the door opened.

As the teacher entered the room he spoke, "Alright students, story time is over, let's get back to work."

Everyone groaned that they wouldn't hear the end of the story.

After graduating from college, I moved away from Syria and came to America where, later on, I got a job that required traveling.

I worked for a company that assigned me to go back to the Middle East including Syria to promote their products.

One day in Damascus City, I had to wait in a very long, slow-moving line. While I was waiting, I noticed one of the workers behind the window was staring at me.

It worried me as I didn't recognize him at all.

When that worker was done with the person he was helping, he left his desk and walked towards me.

He was in his mid-thirties, with a little bit of white in his hair and wrinkles on his face, just like me.

I didn't know what I had done to catch his attention or why he was coming towards me.

He then noticed that I was worried, so he smiled.

USE
ME

"Tarif, is that you?"

I looked carefully into the man's face, trying to remember where I knew him from. He noticed I was at a loss so he said his name and added, "Shame on you for not remembering your Elementary School friend."

After hearing his name, I reacted. "Oh my, I haven't seen you in, what? Thirty years?"

We hugged and then he invited me back to his office and ordered a soft drink for me; I learned that he was the office director.

Holiday
Bali

After a little bit of catching up and discussing the business that I was there for, he looked at my paperwork and spoke.

"The good news is your application looks good." To me, that was a relief. I was ready to thank him and leave when he laughed and spoke again.

"Not so fast my friend, I gave you the good news, but you didn't ask me about the bad news."

Worried, I tried to half-laugh and asked, "Okay, what is the bad news?"

What my friend said after that left me speechless. I was absolutely not expecting to hear this, not even in my wildest dreams.

He said, "I'll approve your papers ONLY if you tell me what happened to *Aziza*."

Puzzled, I looked into his eyes and tried to remember what he was talking about.

When he noticed that I had no clue, he added, "Don't you remember that cold winter morning when our teacher left the classroom and you told us a story?"

When he saw that I was still confused, he added "That day you started the story of *Hassan the Magnificent* and his flying rug *Aziza*. *Aziza* was trying to save her master, when she caught fire from a seven-headed fire breathing serpent."

I understood what he meant, now, but I didn't remember the exact story. I made those adventures up all of the time.

"Oh my goodness," I laughed, "Do you really still remember those stories?"

"I do! And I've been waiting on the edge of my seat to find out what happened to *Aziza* and her master, *Hassan the Magnificent,* for nearly thirty years! So you are not going anywhere until you finish that story!"

"Why didn't you come to me back then and ask about it?" I asked with shock.

He said "I wanted to, but my family moved into another neighborhood and I had to change school. I didn't see you after that. But as a kid, I couldn't forget the story and *Aziza* catching fire, and I always wanted to know the conclusion. It sounds crazy, doesn't it?"

My friend then added with a smile, "I forgot about the whole thing, until I saw you today, and it came rushing back to me."

ZZzz
ZZZ

What amazed me the most was to learn that certain stories could never leave the memory of a child, no matter how many years pass by.

After we talked a bit more, and thinking about my characters, I decided to grant his wish for the end of the story. I woke my imagination up and brought *Aziza* and the Monsters back to life.

"Do you really want to hear what happened to *Aziza*? Are you ready for the last episode of that never-ending adventure?"

He looked at me and smiled, "Go ahead, Your Majesty the Story Teller, my ears are all yours".

I said, "*Aziza* did what anyone would do when a fire starts; she called the Fire Station. The Fire fighters arrived and put out the fire. With their help, they captured the seven-headed serpent, took it to the city zoo and taught it that playing with fire is dangerous.

Soon after *Aziza* saved *Hassan the Magnificent*, the police arrived and restrained the Ghoul. They told him that eating people was not nice, not to mention that it was not healthy, so the Ghoul ended up becoming a vegetarian."

At first, my friend stared at me in full silence. Then, after a few moments, he cracked up laughing.

"Oh Tarif, you really haven't been changed a bit, and you deserve two thumbs up for that ending."

That day I not only remembered the adventures of my childhood stories, I learned about the magical power of story-telling and the lasting memories it can leave on a person's soul.

Especially the effect it can have when it comes to children and their imaginations.

# The Author at a Glance
Tarif Youssef-Agha
www.AuthorAgha.com

Tarif was born in Damascus, Syria in 1957. He started writing short stories and articles in his early years of elementary school and free style poetry in his college years.

He earned 2 BS degrees in Engineering and Literature from Damascus University.

He decided that Syria was not a safe country to live in, so he moved to the U.S. in the Eighties and restarted his life from scratch.

He organized several poetry recitals in Houston in the years 2009 and 2010. As soon as the Arab Spring revolutions started late 2010, he instantly moved to their side where he published 3 books in poetry documenting them and one in short stories describing life under dictatorship.

In 2018, he published his 5th book 'Hearts, Tears and the Journey of Life' that contains collective poems of Love, Lamenting and Meditation.

In 2020, he published his first children book "A Tale of Seven Phones" which blew the whistle about the young generation's addiction to smart phones.

His next book, "What's Special About Judy" gives children the magical secret about how to become SPECIAL. And in THIS book, he shares a true story from his own life that details how important a child's imagination is and how important children's stories are, to young and old. Read to your children. Instill a desire for reading and you will instill a desire for greatness and possibility throughout their entire life.

www.Authoragha.com
https://www.facebook.com/authoragha
https://sites.google.com/site/tarifspoetry/home